MW01618135

Everyday Blessings

By Tracy A. George

Illustrated By Erika Jones

Information requests will be received at www.thankyoubaby.com

ISBN 0-9785767-0-5

The illustrations in this book were done in ink and paint.

Text editing by Julie Roach. Formatting and cover design by Katie Arndt.

Thank You Baby, Inc. is the parent company of Thank You Baby LLC.

Before God had blessed me with you,

I used to feel there were so many things
I had to do!

13
Meetings
dinner 6
Work
14
8-5
No Rest
15
Work all day
around
16
Work out
the clock
nference
meeting
siness
ne call
onference
all-day
ease!
work!
list!
list!
LIST
LIST
Work
job
heavy
burden
BILLS

Running around frantically
just to get things done,
not allowing myself
to have any fun.

Picking up messes before I would stop and sit
just to enjoy the change in scenery even for a little bit.

Since you've arrived I've learned to look around,

Not to hurry so much,
to take my time and slow down

Because...

someday I will miss the floors full of toys,

The laughs, the cries, and all of the noise,

The food thrown all over your face,

The dirt you grabbed and then you ate,

STP'N NJOY

Trips to the park
and all the fun rides --
horses, merry-go-rounds,
swings, and slides,

Crayons, markers,
finger paints, chalk,

Rides in the wagon around the block,

Discovering insects for the first time --

Ladybugs, bees, and butterflies,

The faces you made
when you would sniff
the flowers you found
and then you picked,

The castles we built in the sand

And all the prints left with your little hands,

The times you rested your head on my chest
just to sit and snuggle while you took a rest.

You've taught me to stop and enjoy everything,

Each and every moment
and all that life brings --

Because messes clean up
and tears fade away,
but you can never go back
and relive today.

I thank you baby for showing me all of this,

For without you,
imagine what I would miss!

Primary thanks to the Lord, who truly holds the copyright to this book - He has drawn up some amazing plans! We thank Him for bringing us together and for lifting us up. To the local Gibbon and Kearney communities, friends, teachers, and mentors - you have forever touched our lives. We're still smiling. Special thanks to Marilyn for the very meaningful introduction. The pieces finally fit into place!

- Tracy & Erika

To my biggest fans, my family - you are truly "everyday blessings!" Thank you mom, my strength; dad, my inspiration; Aubs, my joy; and Emma, my dog. You spoil me with endless encouragement. Tracy, thank you for inspiring me always. Your giving spirit amazes me! There will never come a day that I don't have a good cry-fest after reading the beautiful words you have written. Brandon, you are my best friend. Thanks for keeping it real for me, Nanner. I love you all. This is for you!

- Erika

To my most precious of God's gifts and my inspiration, my daughter, Michayla. To my father for his support, love, and strength. To my mother for her courage, confidence, and motivation. To my sister for her never-ending friendship, trust, and faith always! None of this would have been possible without you. To my dogs Turner and Hooch for their protection, friendship and unconditional love. I love you all forever and always. To my lifetime friend and illustrator, Erika, for bringing life to my words - more than I ever dreamed possible! You are a true gift from God.

- Tracy